Taking Time Out
Recreation and Play

======= ✳ =======

CESAR CHAVEZ HIGH SCHOOL
8501 Howard
Houston, Texas 77017

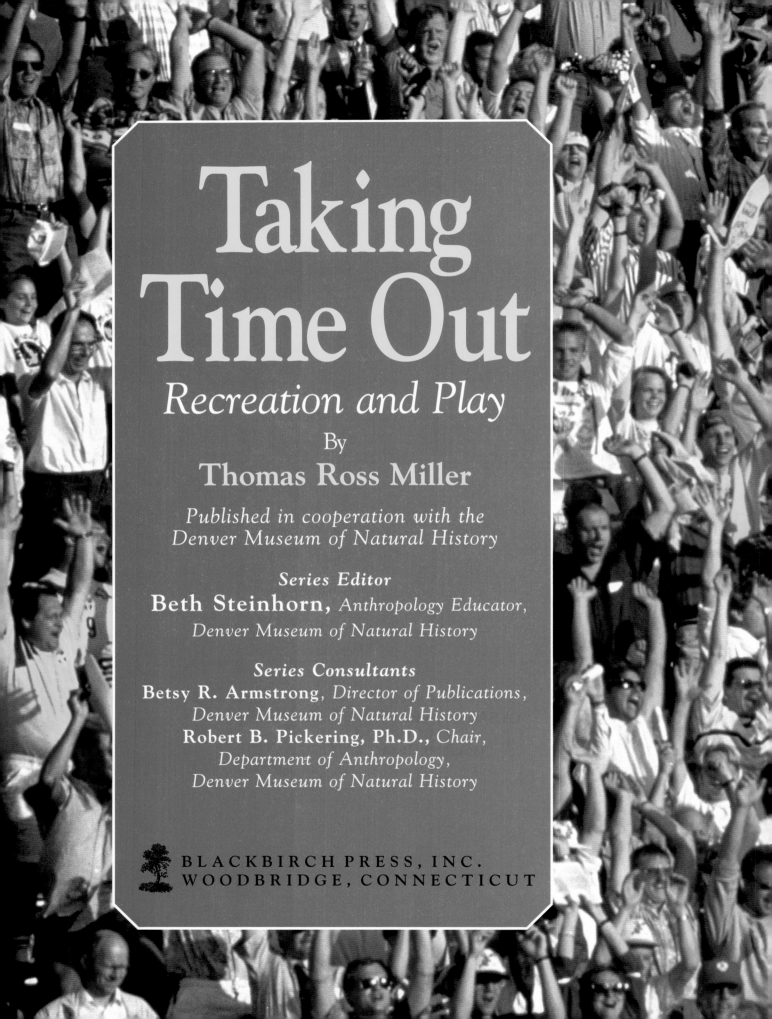

Taking Time Out
Recreation and Play

By
Thomas Ross Miller

*Published in cooperation with the
Denver Museum of Natural History*

Series Editor
Beth Steinhorn, *Anthropology Educator,
Denver Museum of Natural History*

Series Consultants
Betsy R. Armstrong, *Director of Publications,
Denver Museum of Natural History*
Robert B. Pickering, Ph.D., *Chair,
Department of Anthropology,
Denver Museum of Natural History*

BLACKBIRCH PRESS, INC.
WOODBRIDGE, CONNECTICUT

* On the cover: A young boy from Guadeloupe, West Indies, relishes a refreshing swim (© Gerard Del Vecchio/Tony Stone Worldwide).

* On the title page: A French crowd of fans cheers the action at a soccer game (© Gouvernour-Sampers/Gamma-Liaison).

Published by Blackbirch Press, Inc.
260 Amity Road
Woodbridge, CT 06525

©1996 Blackbirch Press, Inc.

Printed in Hong Kong.

10 9 8 7 6 5 4 3 2 1

Blackbirch Press, Inc.

Editorial Director: Bruce S. Glassman
Editor: Lisa Clyde Nielsen
Production Editor: Laura E. Specht
Photo Research: Ellen Cibula

Denver Museum of Natural History:

Photo Research Assistant: Carol R. Weiskopf
Photo Archivist: Liz Clancy
Administrative Assistant: Mary Bushbaum

Library of Congress Cataloging-in-Publication Data

Miller, Thomas Ross.
    Taking time out: recreation and play / by Thomas Ross Miller. — 1st ed.
        p.   cm. — (Our human family)
    "Published in cooperation with the Denver Museum of Natural History"
    Includes bibliographical references and index.
    ISBN 1–56711–128–9 (lib. bdg.)
    1. Games—Social aspects—Juvenile literature. 2. Play—Social aspects—Juvenile literature. 3. Leisure—Social aspects—Juvenile literature. I. Denver Museum of Natural History. II. Title. III. Series.
GV1201.38.M55   1996
306.4'81—dc20   94–47412
                                                              CIP
                                                              AC

Contents

Introduction

As we neared the end of an exciting journey through Turkey, my traveling companion and I stood at the back of a commuter ferry and sailed up the Bosporus Strait, away from the capital city of Istanbul. As the boat chugged away, we soaked up the comforting sight of the cozy three- and four-story row houses that lined the shores. The ferry zigzagged across the narrow Bosporus, stopping frequently to unload passengers, and we caught sight of two young girls staring wide-eyed at us. Both my friend and I immediately assumed the girls were sisters—their matching brown hair and deep brown eyes gave them away. The older one—about thirteen—smiled and, without saying a word, held out a crumpled bag of pistachio nuts in a universal gesture of friendship. Tickled, my friend and I accepted and, in return, offered the girls a handful of chocolate candy we kept stashed in our packs for just such an occasion.

Over the next hour, we and many other passengers were entertained as the girls presided over a floating language classroom, designed to teach us the essentials of Turkish: *lüften* ("please"), *feribot* ("ferry"), and, of course, *fistik* ("pistachio nut"). They also offered a small geography lesson as they pointed out their town on the map. In return, we pulled out a map and pointed to our towns—worlds away, or so it seemed. Soon the younger sister—about seven—took my hand and led us down below to where a group of women were unpacking lunches from their bags. We did our best to introduce ourselves, stumbling in Turkish, laughing a little, smiling a lot. Clearly these were our young friends' mother and aunts—and they were as friendly and gracious as could be. By the time the ferry approached their stop, my companion and I had relished tastes of dates, figs, and börek—the popular and tasty spinach pastries. In return, they had enjoyed listening to our small gifts of American jazz tapes. Before we parted, we exchanged addresses so that we could send copies of the pictures we had taken of each other. Finally, as all good mothers would, the women made sure that my friend and I knew which bus to take back to the city. They even gave us bus tickets in case we didn't have the correct coins.

As we rode back to Istanbul, I marveled at how two groups of people from such disparate cultures could meet and, in just an hour, bridge oceans of differences in order to become friends. How had we managed—with so few words and common experiences—to communicate, laugh, share lunch, and even decide that we actually liked each other? A few years later—on a beach halfway around the world—another encounter brought these thoughts rushing back.

It was during an expedition to the cold, foggy tip of a Siberian peninsula that I met other children, this time gathered, curious, as we stepped off our boat and onto the rocky beach of their small village. A few adults stood watching, more cautious, at the edge of a cluster of grey, peeling buildings that were barely visible from shore.

As I stood facing a handful of ten- to twelve-year-old Siberian boys, I was immediately struck by the obstacles that seemed to stand between us: We didn't speak the same language; we knew virtually nothing about each other; and we had only a few hours before our ship continued its journey northbound.

Our first attempts at communication were the obvious hand signals and smiles, but we met little success. Then one of the boys discreetly pulled a small hidden treasure from his pocket, and the others quickly followed suit. Within seconds, our group was presented with a wonderful variety of items, including a collection of carved animals in bone and ivory, small leather pouches trimmed with seal fur, and a rock of a particularly interesting shape. All these treasures were being held out to us for sale or trade, a universal language that all my fellow travelers understood immediately.

Meanwhile, one boy pulled me aside and proudly demonstrated his handmade sling shot. As he aimed at a fence, cans on the beach, and an unfortunate team of dogs chained to a nearby post, he gave me a no-frills lesson in Siberian sling-shot technique.

It had been only twenty or thirty minutes since our arrival, but by the time we all walked up the beach together, we had become at least short-term friends. When we reached town, the boys enthusiastically introduced us to their families. Naturally, we took out photos of our families and offered views in return. We then traded a few modest trinkets and, before we departed, were given a guided tour of the village museum. There we caught glimpses of the spectacular ivory carvings that make the artists of this particular village famous.

In both the bustling outskirts of Istanbul and the remote Siberian village, I came face to face with young people from worlds vastly different from my own. In each case, we were separated by different languages, customs, and lifestyles. Both times, however, curiosity, a desire to learn, and a shared sense of friendship, family, and fun enabled us to bring our worlds together for a brief time.

The memories I have of Turkey and Siberia—as well as others like them—come to my mind often as I work in museums, study anthropology collections, and teach others about cultures. These are recollections I hold particularly dear because, above all, they remind me of what it really means to be human. They prove that, even though people may appear very different on the surface, our differences all grow out of the same basic needs. They grow out of needs that all humans share: the need to communicate; to create and appreciate beauty; to learn; even the need to play and have fun.

All of these needs connect us. What makes us different is how each group of people develops its own unique answers to these needs. Together, their answers create a unique way of life, a pattern we call culture. But, underneath the patterns on the surface—whether we live in a big-city apartment or dwell in a desert tent—we remain linked by our common needs. These needs, and the human spirit that enables us to fulfill them, bind us together into one "human family."

Beth Steinhorn
Anthropology Educator
Denver Museum of Natural History

1

People at Play

Twenty-five children hold hands and turn in a circle. But one child—the "mouse"—stands inside the circle, while another—the "cat"—stands outside. Suddenly the turning stops. The cat runs in one side and the mouse runs out another. They dart in and out of the circle, the cat following the mouse's path until the mouse is caught. Then a new cat and a new mouse are chosen, and the game begins all over again.

This particular game of "cat and mouse" is played in China. But people everywhere play—whether it's in a neighborhood soccer match in Brazil, a dance party in Africa, or a chess tournament in Russia. Some **games are casual and** played just for fun, while others are highly organized contests that are played for money or prestige.

✳ Opposite: Kids in Madrid, Spain, enjoy a game of soccer in the Plaza de Colon.

9

The Frame of the Game

The urge to play is something deep within us all, no matter what our age or ethnic background. Children can play without being taught. Yet there are as many different ways to play as there are people. Looking at the ways that people in different cultures play will help to answer the central question of this book: Why do people all over the world play?

There are body games and mind games, team games and games played alone, games of skill and games of chance. Some games—like soccer, tennis, or basketball—depend on athletic skills. Others are mind games: riddles, puzzles, brain-teasers, counting games, and word games. Some games are played with balls, dice, cards, or boards, while others exist only in the imagination. Some of the games we play are as old as humankind itself, others are the latest fad, and still others may be made up on the spot. Games can be played for points, against a clock, or until the players get tired or bored. Some games, like the

✳ Baseball players in Tokyo, Japan, practice their skills.

* Two gentlemen in New York City's Central Park concentrate on an outdoor game of chess.

lottery, depend entirely on chance, while others, like chess, are games of pure skill and strategy. Most games involve some combination of ability and luck.

Games, which have been around for as long as humans have existed, have rules and are structured ways to play. Games may be played in a special area, such as a playground, or in an everyday setting like a living room. A game must have at least one player, and usually has some set of rules. A common type of game is the battle between two opposing sides, with individuals having personal loyalties to one side or the other. This type of game is most often played until one side wins and the other loses.

Many team sports, like basketball and football, are played against a clock. These games usually have clear out-of-bounds markers, team huddles, and a certain number of "time-outs" allowed to each side. Baseball is an unusual sport, in that the field has no standard dimensions (each ballpark is a different size and shape) and no clock (play continues until one side wins). In some sports, such as baseball and football, most of the time is actually spent between plays; the game itself is played in short bursts of intense activity, with longer periods of inactivity in between. In other sports, like basketball, soccer, and hockey, play is more or less continuous.

Games mirror society, which also operates by a set of rules known as laws and customs. In a game, there may be a referee, or spectators may serve as eyewitnesses and judges. Players or officials may stop the game momentarily. In sports, referees keep score and decide what counts and what doesn't. They penalize or discipline players, and try to ensure fairness. In the "real world," lawyers and judges discipline and exact fairness in courts, and public opinion serves as a powerful arbiter of justice.

What Is Play?

Play is something we all know and do, yet it is not easy to define. One hallmark of play is that it is often an activity done just for its own sake, for no other reason than having fun. Yet, as we shall see, play can also have serious and important purposes.

Many players make a commitment to the specific rules of a game, and make their own choices within it. Play can be relaxing, but it can also create tensions that arise specifically from the game itself. This tension is usually released at the end of a game when the outcome is decided and the winners and losers accept the results of their performances. The effort and struggle that are associated with victory and defeat may be taken as

✳ Kids in Listvyanka, Siberia, put the finishing touches on a snowman.

signs of a person's—or group's—qualities. The winners are often seen as possessing strength, endurance, determination, skill, intelligence, and dedication. The losers—if they lose with grace— may be perceived as unlucky, dignified, or even courageous.

While every culture has its own unique kinds of play, versions of the oldest, most familiar kinds of play, or games, are found all over the world. "Hide and seek," for example, is one of the most basic and universal games known. It takes many forms, from an infant's "peek-a-boo" to highly elaborate scavenger hunts, to "blind man's bluff,"—a kind of hide-and-seek in which no one actually hides but the seeker is blindfolded. On Little Andaman Island in the Indian Ocean, Ongee children play a version of "hide and seek" called *gukwelonone*. This game, which kids play just for fun, teaches them how to hunt and fight by concealing themselves or sneaking up on their opponents and flushing them out.

Tag is another type of game that has found its way into many diverse cultures—from the popular Asian game of *kabbadi* to "freeze tag" and "TV tag" in America. Other games and athletic events, such as javelin throwing, archery, and marksmanship are based on important hunting skills. Many rough-and-tumble sports, such as wrestling, imitate combat and build combat skills.

Many well-known competitive games began as imitations of warfare. Athletic contests and board games alike are often battles between opposing sides for territory or points. Some of our most familiar games, from chess to red rover, are patterned after military models with two opposing sides battling for territory. Many of the world's most popular video games are high-stress obstacle courses that require quick thinking and razor sharp reflexes—just the survival skills needed in today's high-tech age. The rules and styles of play in these games reflect their strategic origins. The fast-moving game of *baggataway*, played as both a competitive sport and a religious ritual, was an important form of training for Native-American warriors. The Iroquois called the game "the little brother of war;" today it is known as lacrosse. In ancient MesoAmerica, a ball game was sometimes played by two opposing cities in place of fighting a war.

✳ Two Japanese youngsters face off during a sumo wrestling contest in the city of Seki.

Whether it's a competition, a puzzle, or imaginary role-playing, the act of play helps to prepare children for adult life, and sharpens or challenges the skills that adults have already acquired. In addition, play provides a safe outlet for aggression and energy.

When we play, we willingly enter into a world of imagination—a world different from the "real" world of everyday life. The world of play is a special one, with its own rules and rituals. In games, we behave differently than we do in the "real" world. A game depends on players agreeing to go along with predetermined rules, by allowing the world of the game to be "real" for a set period of time. The world of play is exciting: In an instant, an underdog can suddenly become a hero, a seemingly hopeless situation can turn into a sweet victory. In the world of play, players can go as far as their imagination and skill will take them.

Why We Play

People everywhere, young and old, play for many different reasons. Among the most universal reasons are the facts that: 1) play is social; 2) play helps us to learn; and 3) play is enjoyable. These three elements are the keys to understanding why we play.

Play Is Social

Play is one of the most basic ways in which people interact. You can play alone, but many games can only be played with others. Social play includes dances and group activities as well as team sports and contests. Many common forms of social play center around competition. Fair play is "sportsmanlike": it is an honorable quality that all players are expected to exhibit. "Poor sports" are looked down upon by their peers—they are often criticized for not extending the common courtesies of play to others.

Because play is social, it reflects the society in which we live. In organized recreation, certain pastimes are associated with certain social groupings. For example, historically, upper-class games like golf, tennis, or polo may provide a player with social status and business connections as well as pleasure. Local football teams or pickup basketball games can give players a pleasurable feeling of belonging to a group of friends within a neighborhood, and a sense of fair competition with rivals outside. Though they provide challenges and the thrill of competition, some athletic contests can become very serious indeed, as certain elements of the "real" world seep into the supposedly "imagined" world of the game. Usually, though, games and sports provide a safe arena for friendly alliances as well as hostile rivalries—most players follow the rules, with few people getting hurt. Often the friendly bonds of competition forged in play carry over into the business world and social life. Games teach and utilize valuable adult skills such as cooperation, leadership, diplomacy, strategy, cleverness, and trying to work successfully within a set of rules.

All Animals Play

✳ Two squirrel monkeys play together in a tree.

Play is a behavior common not only to human children but also to other young animals. Puppies, kittens, monkeys, and other growing mammals tumble, wrestle, chase each other, and engage in mock fights. By mimicking adults, baby animals learn important skills such as hunting and grooming. Through play, young humans and other animals explore the world around them, testing and improving their physical abilities, learning to solve problems, and developing ways to interact with their peers. They also gain many specific skills they will need in order to survive as adults, such as hunting and defending territory.

One of the mysteries of animal behavior is how animals distinguish between play and non-play. Kittens attack their brothers and sisters with seemingly ferocious leaps and pounces, claws and teeth bared. Despite this, they don't hurt each other as they would in a real fight. Researchers are still trying to discover the signals that tell an animal, "This is only play."

Monkeys, like humans and other primates, play in highly specialized ways, learning to use tools, and forming social bonds and friendships through group interaction. Much of a young rhesus monkey's waking life is spent in one of two kinds of play. One is "rough-and-tumble" or monkey wrestling matches, in which—despite fierce biting and scratching—no animal gets hurt. The second is a game resembling tag that scientists call "approach-avoidance," in which the monkeys chase each other but have little physical contact. Females will play more "approach-avoidance" while males tend to play more "rough-and-tumble." As the monkeys get older, their play becomes more aggressive and begins to mirror adult mating patterns.

From about nine months to three years of age, rhesus monkeys start to play less and behave more like adults. Fully grown monkeys play occasionally, particularly mothers playing with their infants. Fathers may act as referees in games played by their young, joining in the action once in a while.

Scientific research in animal behavior has shown just how important play is in the social and emotional development of primates. Rhesus monkeys who are raised apart from other monkeys, and thus without playmates, grow up to be severely disturbed. They can perform intellectual tasks but cannot function in monkey society. Without the experiences of play, they have missed out on the most important early behaviors of rhesus life (social grooming, aggression, dominance, and mating). The deprived monkeys never learn to channel and control aggression in acceptable ways, or to take part in a social group. Researchers agree that the results seen in rhesus monkeys would be almost identical for humans and other primates.

✳ Elephants in Kenya rub each other playfully.

✳ Teenage girls in New York City, United States, practice their "double Dutch" jumprope routine.

Play Helps Us to Learn

Play is useful. In fact, it is one of the first activities of all human beings. During play, a child learns and develops. When babies first open their eyes and begin to move, one of their earliest actions is to play. Rattles, balls, or dangling strings amuse and delight. As infants reach out to grasp these objects, they make contact with the world outside themselves. They explore their surroundings, getting acquainted with colors, shapes, and textures through playful experimentation.

Play also stimulates early learning. When children play, they learn by doing simple tasks, solving problems, developing memory and logic, role-playing, and using imagination. They develop physical and mental abilities, and practice in mastering adult skills. Play has been called "the mother of culture," because we play before we learn to speak or behave in ways specific to our parents' world. As we grow up, we learn to play in ways that fit the society we live in.

One of the main ways we learn is through imitation, a learning process we share with many other animals. Children play by imitating the adults they see around them, creating their own versions of the grown-up world. As they imitate and repeat what adults do, they learn about work, cooperation, and human relationships in their society. They act out the parts of "mommy" and "daddy," play with dolls, drive toy trucks, or use miniature tools. However, children do not simply decide for themselves which roles to take on. To a major degree, society does this for them, by having gender-based social expectations and, thus, different games, toys, and rules for boys and girls. Because gender roles are not the same in every society, each culture has developed its own process for how and what young children play. In this way, the values of each culture are reflected in the games played by its youngest members.

Play Is Enjoyable

In many cases, play is not intended for learning or skill building. Much of the time, people play for simple fun and excitement, for pleasure, or for relaxation. The world of play is a special world because, in the end, all the "work" of play demands no "real" result. While we learn skills and interact socially during play, the main point is often just to have fun. When we play just for fun, we need no other reason—and need not have anything to show at the end.

Ancient Games

Many of the world's most popular and widespread games have their roots in ancient cultures. Humans have apparently played marbles for thousands of years, using stones, nuts, or other round objects. Other games using balls, such as billiards and pool, are closely related to marbles. So is bowling, which was popular more than 7,000 years ago in Egypt as well as in ancient Greece, Rome, and Polynesia. In the Americas, the ancient Mayans and Aztecs played *tlachtli*, a game similar to modern-day soccer.

The Play's the Thing

Play-acting is also playing; it is play that is often done for the entertainment or recreation of others. In a dramatic performance, a make-believe world of the imagination replaces our everyday reality. Whether it's a simple game of dress-up at home or a show put on in a theater, pretending is governed not by a set of rules but by a formula: character, setting, and situation. In creative play you use your imagination freely, improvising situations, characters, and events. When you pretend, you make up your own world and freely choose roles.

Babies take up role-playing early on, when they mimic their parents and other adults. Toddlers like to imitate the sounds of animals they see and hear, and like to explore and play with other objects in everyday life.

Play-acting is generally non-competitive and flexible, although it still depends on agreement among the players. The roles may be based on a model from stories, movies, or real life. In the made-up world of fiction and fantasy games, a child may even pretend to be an actor or a movie star, who in turn pretends to be a made-up character.

Whether in a formal play on a stage, or a made-up game on the playground, role-playing is a useful and entertaining escape from daily reality. It is also educational. When we play a character, we try to act and think as that person would. This process takes us out of ourselves and opens our minds to the world of others.

Chariot racing, a forerunner of horse racing and auto racing, was popular in the ancient world. Wrestling and other contests of strength and agility were other ancient favorites, reaching great heights of mass appeal during the Greek and Roman empires. Dominoes, most likely a Chinese invention of the seventeenth century, may have entered Europe via Italy. Cards, which made their way into Europe from the Far East about 700 years ago, were at first used more for fortune-telling than for games. Dice, which are related to Chinese dominoes, are a popular element in gambling, which is another ancient and popular pastime, found in widely different societies.

Sports and games were played enthusiastically in ancient Egypt, generally in private rather than in front of a crowd. Children and adults participated in many athletic contests including running, jumping, and whirling. The oldest sports facility in the world is the stone running track at the Pyramid of Joser, built some 4,600 years ago in Egypt. In the hot desert summer, adults sat in the shade and played board games. The most popular game was Senet, played with stone pieces and bone dice on a board of thirty squares. Another ancient Egyptian favorite was the Snake Game, in which players most likely threw sticks to move six lion-shaped pieces along a spiral board that was shaped like a snake.

✳ The ancient Mayan ball game was similar to present-day soccer and was played by highly respected athletes. Inset: The remains of an ancient ball-court in Monte Alban, Mexico.

In ancient Greece, taking part in athletics was prized as an important part of being a well-rounded citizen. Many of our modern track-and-field events, including the discus, javelin, decathlon, and marathon have ancient Greek origins, as do the Olympic Games themselves. The staging of these sporting contests before giant crowds of spectators can also be traced back to the Greeks. When the Roman Empire succeeded the Greeks, many of these traditions were passed on and expanded.

In Europe during the Middle Ages, jousting tournaments were a form of recreation that involved people from all walks of life, from knights to stable-boys. During these colorful spectacles, competitive knights charged and lanced each other in ferocious battles. Some fell while others tried to rescue them and turn back the attack. These violent pageants established rankings among the nobility while they entertained the masses.

Many common games, played just for fun today, originally began as ceremonies with other specific meanings. In the early springtime, for example, people used to go out looking for birds, flowers, or insects to show the change of seasons. Others would hide in the woods and imitate birds, trying in a good-natured way to throw the seekers off the trail. Over the centuries, this ritual that marked the beginning of spring became the familiar game we now know as "hide and seek." Today, wherever versions of hide and seek are played around the world, the players have developed certain special elements of the game that make it uniquely their own.

Work, Play, Recreation, and Leisure

Mark Twain's Tom Sawyer said that "work consists of whatever a body is obliged to do.... Play consists of whatever a body is not obliged to do." Yet people are often happiest when they have a job they can enjoy; in other words, when they can turn some of their work into play. The separation of work and play is by no means universal. In fact, the English word *school* comes from the ancient Greek word *scholé*, meaning "leisure!" The separation of "work" and "play" was not generally made until fairly recent times. In many cultures, children and adults play in their everyday life, but do not think of the activity of playing games as separate from their work. Other people, such as Alaskan Eskimo children, set time aside for play but have few organized games.

The line between work and play is not always clear. Games can be hard work, as anyone who has gone through training for a sports team knows. The play of toddlers may include imitating adults at work. When we invent games to make our chores easier or more pleasant, we turn work into a kind of play. For example, occupational games and work songs can make a hard job easier by focusing attention differently, providing a rhythm, and relieving the drudgery of repetitive tasks. In Japan, employees exercise together and sing company songs as part of their daily routine. For the Japanese, a corporation is like a family, and these group activities are meant to help keep workers perpetually healthy, productive, and loyal.

Through the years, as modern industry developed, working hours grew longer, more rigidly defined, and more repetitive. Leisure and sport, as special activities outside of the daily working routine, became more valued as an antidote to the burdens of modern industrial civilization. The quest for organized activities to promote health and happiness created many ways to relax, including national parks, scouting, and amateur sports leagues. Today, organized recreation is an important part of life in many countries. We have active forms of leisure, like skiing, and tourism, as well as passive forms, like movies and spectator sports. New forms of interactive electronic leisure, such as video and computer games, combine the active and the passive.

As we explore the world of play, games, and leisure in the chapters that follow, think about the ways in which play is a universal human activity, yet is different in every culture. That aspect is what makes the act of playing so rich and fascinating. Through play, children and adults everywhere learn, interact socially, and have fun. Play is a human quality that we all share, yet one that each of us expresses in our own unique ways. The endless variety of games people play reveals human diversity, creativity, and the joy of living.

2

The Americas

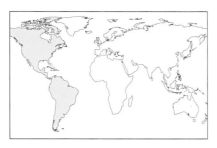

The Americas were settled count-less generations before Columbus arrived some 500 years ago. In the last Ice Age, the Bering Strait between Alaska and Siberia was frozen solid. At least 15,000 years ago (no one knows exactly when), the first Americans came over this land bridge from Asia. Over the centuries, people spread throughout the western hemisphere. Native-American societies flourished for thousands of years, from small bands of hunter-gatherers in the subarctic regions to the huge Toltec, Aztec, and Mayan empires of ancient Mexico. In the later European conquests, from Mexico and the Caribbean in the six-teenth century to the American west in the nineteenth century, the great majority of Native Americans were killed in battle or

✳ Opposite: Players compete in a fast-paced game of volleyball on a beach in California, United States.

fell victim to European diseases. But the Native Americans did not disappear—many of their cultures are very much alive today. Although life has changed drastically in the past century, old traditions are being revived by Native Americans who are reclaiming their heritage.

In both Central and South America, native peoples have traditionally maintained a stronger cultural presence over the centuries. In many areas, they have mixed equally with the Spanish immigrants to create *mestizo* (mixed) cultures. Different areas of the Americas were colonized by Spain, England, France, and Portugal. North, Central, and South Americans took on the languages and many other aspects of culture of their colonizers. Yet in each country the people evolved a distinct cultural identity. The islands of the Caribbean, for example, which include Cuba, Haiti, Jamaica, and many others are populated largely by people of African descent. Their ancestors were forcibly brought to the Americas in the slave trade. Based on African roots, Native-American ideas and European overlays, each island group developed a unique culture and style.

Immigrants from all parts of the world have blended throughout the Americas, creating many thriving cultures. For more than three hundred years, waves of immigrants have come to North America to build a new life. There, Europeans, Native Americans, Asians, Africans, and others have created a flourishing and vibrant mix of cultures that have influenced the world.

Kinds of Play: Hand Games, Stick Games, and Ball Games

Among the many games developed by North American Indians, some of the most popular are games of concealment and games of chance. At large gatherings, "stick games" and "hand games" are especially important. Stick games are a form of guessing game where one player will hold a bundle of sticks or bones in each hand as other players guess which hand contains the stick with the mark on it. Hand games are similar; one player hides marked and unmarked stones, sticks, or other small objects in his or her hands and the other players guess which hand is holding what. Both varieties are games of concealment and chance, but stick games are played mostly for recreation and sporting competition, while hand games are more ceremonial. Stick games are more common in the western United States, while hand games are more popular in the east.

Lacrosse, a game that began as an imitation of warfare, developed into a highly organized tournament sport and became internationally popular in the nineteenth and twentieth centuries. Using curved sticks, players on a large field attempt to hurl a ball into their opponents' net. The wide-open traditional game played by Iroquois and Choctaw may have been something like the Turkish game *holani*. In the seventeenth century and earlier, woodland tribes gathered for lacrosse matches that usually lasted for two or three days and could involve hundreds

✳ The ancient Native-American game of lacrosse is played in the Americas today on the college, professional, and international levels.

of players. Canadian settlers adopted the game, naming it after the curved stick, which they called "the crosse." Today, some of the best lacrosse sticks are still made by American Indians.

Dangerous Games

Tlachtli, the ancient ballgame of the MesoAmericans, is more than 3,500 years old. In Mexico, it was played on magnificent walled ballcourts before large crowds. Using only their knees, hips, and elbows, teams in ceremonial dress battled to keep a rubber ball from touching the ground. The game ended when one player managed to bounce the ball off his body through a stone hoop mounted high on the wall of the ballcourt. Ancient evidence suggests that winners were rewarded with prizes of wealth and glory, while losers were shamed, and on occasion may have been put to death. To give one's life up to Xochipilli, the god of the ballgame, was considered an honor. Some scholars think this noble death was so prized that the winners, not the losers, were sacrificed!

Even if tlachtli was rarely played to the death, the ballgame was no idle pleasure, it was a serious contest for status and prestige. Star players were showered with gifts, and entire kingdoms were wagered on the outcome of the competitions. The ballcourt symbolized the earth, and the ball represented the sun or the moon. At the game's peak, it was played from El Salvador to Arizona and throughout the Caribbean. A nonviolent but competitive ballgame called *ulama*, which is descended from tlachtli, is still played by native peoples in Mexico today.

Blood sport, however, is not just a thing of the past. Today, adults in many parts of the world gather in large crowds to gamble on dog fights or cockfights. Bullfighting, which began in Spain and may have roots in ancient Greece, is a popular sport in Mexico and in some other parts of Latin America. The colorful pageant of the bullfight reaches a climax with the ritual goring of the bull. The triumphant *matador* (bullfighter) is then showered with cheers and presents. If a bull puts up an especially noble fight, however, the sentiment of the crowd may sway the hero to spare the beast.

* Thousands of spectators watch as a matador confronts a bull in the bullfighting arena in Ambato, Ecuador.

Canada's Games on Ice

In Canada, some sports are played on ice during the long winter on frozen lakes and ponds. There is some evidence that hundreds of years ago, North American Indians played a form of ice hockey. Other early forms of ice hockey included the ancient Scottish game of hurley and the game of bandy, widely played from Sweden to Mongolia. Field hockey first began in Iran and was featured in the first Greek Olympiads. In England, field hockey games moved onto the ice in winter.

Legend has it that the modern form of ice hockey was first played in Canada by groups of English soldiers during the 1850s. Originally, teams had nine players to a side, until the 1886 Montreal Winter Carnival, when not enough players showed up. The game they played with seven-member teams proved to be faster and more exciting, and smaller teams became the rule. During the 1880s, field hockey equipment was gradually converted to ice hockey equipment. The rubber ball was sliced off at the ends to become a puck, and the stick was lengthened and given a flatter blade for better handling on the ice. There were no nets; the goal was a post with crossbar. (A rule was made that goalies had to remain standing; otherwise, they could completely block the goal by lying down across it!) By the 1890s, organized ice hockey leagues across Canada were playing for the Stanley Cup.

Today, ice hockey is a high-speed, very rough contact sport. Players skate up to twenty-five miles per hour, with the puck traveling at up to one hundred miles per hour. Penalty rules were established in 1918 to ensure safety and fair play. Canadian teams dominated international competition until the 1950s, when the sport became widely popular in Russia. Today, young Canadian hockey players compete enthusiastically in indoor ice rinks as well as on frozen lakes. As a spectator sport, ice hockey is less popular in the United States than football, basketball, or baseball. But all across Canada, hockey night is a major social event that brings people together to root for their favorite teams, to celebrate victory, or to commiserate in defeat.

Curling, a sport that resembles bowling on ice, is played by more than half a million Canadians. The mechanics look rather awkward at first glance: Players take turns hurling a heavy stone down the ice and rapidly sweeping its path with a broom. The stone is a rounded granite rock weighing about forty pounds, with a handle attached by iron rods. As the stone slides, a player sweeps in front of it with a broom. This bit of work clears frost and dust from the ice, decreasing friction and slightly melting the ice to increase the distance the stone travels before coming to a stop. Two circles called "houses" are drawn on the ice, and the players try to place their stones at the center of their opponents' house. Curlers use a twisting motion to deliver the stone; if its path is smooth, it is said to be "well soled," but if it bounces and wobbles it's called "kiggle-caggle." Players can make the stone follow a curved path by hurling it with a spin or by sweeping in one direction.

✳ Youngsters in Ottawa play a game of ice hockey, one of Canada's most popular sports.

※ Canadian curlers crouch on the ice, moving their stones toward their opponents' "house."

Inuit Games with Sounds

On Hudson Bay, native Inuit play a musical pastime known as *katajjaq*, or the throat game. Two girls, or women, sit facing one another as they rapidly take turns making short, deep, guttural sounds. The words are meaningless, and players can use any combination of sounds—breathing in or out— but must follow specific rhythms. The object of the game is to outlast the other player; the game usually ends in a burst of laughter when one or the other player runs out of breath, misses a beat, is unable to follow the speed or rhythm, or cannot think of a sound to make. Players develop the difficult art of breath control, and mothers use throat-game songs to teach their babies the sounds of language or animal imitations.

Inuit throat games are played for entertainment, and there is no particular emphasis on winning and competition. The rules are flexible, and the fun comes from the two players being evenly balanced. Throat games are played during spring festivals and camp gatherings, and provide an occasion for isolated northerners to visit and socialize with each other.

Action Games

In Argentina, the fast-moving game of *pato* ("duck") is a blend of rugby and polo (or the even wilder horse-and-rider game of *buzkashi*, played in Asia). In the original form of pato, ranchers and cowboys on horseback competed to capture a basket that contained a live duck. The excitement was heightened by their being allowed to lasso one another while riding. Today the sport is organized into team competitions, and a basket-shaped ball is used instead of an unlucky duck.

People adapt games to the environment in which they live. Argentine ranchers used to play pato on a field several miles long, but modern city-dwellers often must make do with an alley or a street. In the United States, city kids play stickball in neighborhood streets. These informal games are often interrupted by passing cars and other distractions. More organized play activities are carried out by school teams, youth leagues, and clubs.

Play Is Social: Courtship and Competition

Play is an important teacher of social skills. Games and competition in an "imaginary" world of play prepare us for winning and losing in real life. Games teach us to take things in stride, to be gracious winners as well as gracious losers. In play, our personalities emerge and are shaped. Some individuals thrive in a tense atmosphere of rigorous competition, while others excel best in a more relaxed setting. Competitive games can often separate weak from strong, fast from slow, leaders from followers—as well as give individuals a way to prove their abilities and overcome these labels. Most everyone wins at something, sometime; but hardly anyone can win at everything, all the time. Competitive, crafty, energetic, or offensive play wins in certain games; cooperative, trustworthy, supportive, or defensive play wins at others. In the process

✳ Young boys in Guatemala crowd together on a playground slide.

✳ City-dwellers in New York, United States, enjoy a neighborhood game of basketball on a concrete court.

of play, children discover and invent their personal styles according to the skills and strategies that each game requires.

Not all games are battles. Courtship has been called the "game of love," and is surely one of the most universally played. From the first nursery rhymes and dress-up games, pairing off into couples and holding pretend marriages are a universal feature of children's play. At parties, teenagers everywhere play organized couple games. Players may be blindfolded or matched up at random, as in "spin the bottle" and "post office." Within the confines of the game, players are not fully responsible for their choices, which relieves embarrassment and peer pressure. Romance is made safer by the presence of the social group and the requirements and rules of the game. Reassured by friends and the structure of the game, teenage players feel more comfortable taking chances and expressing emotions.

In the rural United States, traditional "play-parties" are social gatherings that feature songs, dances, games, and entertainments. These occasions are important because they offer

* Children at a day-care facility in Huayoko, Peru, play the universally popular game of "ring around the rosey."

young people—who may live great distances apart—a chance to interact in a social setting. In Texas, dancing was forbidden by preachers, but young people used to gather in homes to sing songs. Adding movements to the songs, they came up with "games" that resembled square dances. By the early twentieth century, social life revolved around Saturday night play-parties. The play-party gave people a chance to flirt and court as well as dance and have fun. In small American towns to this day, young and old alike swing their partners at play-parties, accompanied by classic songs like "Buffalo Gals," "Rare Back Chicken" and "Skip to My Lou."

Play Helps Us to Learn: Playing Roles

In games and fantasy play, young children learn to play roles by simulating adult behavior. Some role-playing games are based on the everyday rules of society. American games, such as

"Simon says" and "red light, green light," for example, rely on following simple instructions. Other games are based on more adult roles, like "king of the mountain," which is a physical scramble for power and dominance. In fantasy games like "house" and "dress-up," young children imitate mommy and daddy directly, by acting the part.

From a very early age, boys and girls throughout the Americas are taught to be different from each other. It is common for girls to wear pink, play with dolls, and give tea-parties, while boys wear blue, play with toy guns, and pursue rough sports. These, however, are not "natural" differences—no universal law requires that boys "play war" and girls "play house." These roles are given to children by the society in which they live—and they can be often reversed, changed, or even dropped. Adults give children certain toys and games, from which the children learn certain social roles. Through the kinds of games they teach their children to play, societies send powerful messages to children about what kind of adults they are expected to be.

Fun and Leisure: That's Entertainment

The modern idea of "leisure time" developed in England during the nineteenth century, when the work day became more rigid and time-consuming. Before the "industrial revolution," when large factories were first built, people's work and play were a more integral part of daily life. With the development of machinery and industrialization, however, working hours became more structured and predictable. The rhythm of daily life now consisted of long shifts at work and less time at home. To balance new working patterns, maintain healthy exercise, and provide relief from routine, people in industrialized societies developed more organized forms of recreation, such as the creation of the city park or the Sunday outing. In the cities of Canada, America, and South America, as in England, the idea of "free time" outside of work spread. New leisure habits arose, along with new pastimes to fill the hours away from work.

Strings Attached: Kwakiutl String Figures

✳ Kwakiutl string expert, Agnes Cranmer.

String figures (Americans know them as "cat's cradle"), are among the world's most widespread games. Anywhere there is rope, fiber, or tall grass, a strand can be woven into new shapes. Spreading the string between out-stretched fingers, a player executes a series of moves that make geometric pictures. Two players can pass the string back and forth, making new patterns with each turn. Eskimos and American Indians have some of the biggest and most accomplished string-figure repertoires. The Kwakiutl of British Columbia, in western Canada, have more than a hundred such figures. Most have poetic names that describe a picture, animal, mythical being or story. Some movements contain a whole series of variations, such as the "Fish Trap" and "Pulling His Sweetheart's Hair." Other Kwakiutl string figures even depict cultural values, such as "A Kick in the Back," which represents shame. "Laughing in the House" symbolizes amusement and courtship. In "Two Bear Brothers' Jealousy," a large and a small loop trade places, as an overly anxious small brother

jumps past an elder while hunting. Probably the largest group of Kwakiutl figures, though, represents animals important in daily life and the environment such as the porcupine, sparrow, and killer whale. In other parts of the world, most string figures are also named after animals.

✸ Young baseball fans in Minneapolis, Minnesota, United States, crowd a player in hopes of getting an autograph.

Clubs, sporting events, and hobbies were some of these new forms of leisure.

Today, play, recreation, and leisure are big business throughout the Americas. Americans spend an estimated $45 billion dollars a year on sporting equipment alone. In Canada and America combined, hundreds of millions of fans watch professional sporting events, movies, and videos each week. At more than $19 billion dollars a year, Hollywood's entertainment industry is one of the most important elements of America's economy. The search for new and better kinds of entertainment in the Americas is constant. Computer games, interactive movies, and cable television are just a few of the latest popular technologies. In the twentieth century, the invention of movies, the phonograph, the radio, television, and other passive entertainments moved many away from active participation in leisure pursuits. Newer technologies may reverse this long trend of increasingly passive recreation and leisure, as interactive media all over the world now allow us to participate more in our own electronic amusements.

3

Africa

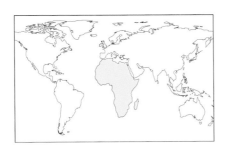

Africa is the second-largest continent in the world. The massive and forbidding Sahara desert cuts across its middle and divides the continent into two giant climatic zones. Northern Africa is largely desert, while the land below the Sahara is varied and includes dense tropical rainforests. Culturally, much of North Africa shares the religion of Islam and other cultural traits with the "Middle Eastern" countries of southwestern Asia. Much of this common culture can be traced back more than a thousand years, when Arabs first established towns on the eastern coast of the continent and then moved north.

Subsaharan Africa is home to hundreds of different peoples with diverse cultures, ways of life, and a wide variety of spoken languages. Since the fifteenth century, when Europeans first appeared on the continent, a great many influences have shaped

39

✳ Berber teenagers in Morocco play a game of leapfrog.

the lifestyles and cultures of Africa. The Portuguese, who first landed on Africa's western shores in 1441; the Spanish, who began trading in earnest from the continent during the late 1400s; the Dutch, who first appeared in southern Africa in 1652, only to be followed by trading concerns of Swedish, Danish, German, French, and English origins; all these European presences made their everlasting mark on the history of Africa.

Kinds of Play: Games and Toys

The factory-made toys and games that Canadians and Americans buy are not available in much of the world. In Africa, manufactured products are hard to come by, but there is plenty of ingenious creativity. Kpelle children in Liberia, for example, have few store-bought toys, but any ordinary object they play with becomes a toy. Whereas toys in many parts of the Americas are made by toy companies and bought by parents, most African toys are made by children, for children. Making the most of whatever they can find, young African builders skillfully recycle old materials in clever ways. From leftover wire, odd bits of rubber and string, empty tin cans, and discarded pieces of fabric, children will make working model cars, trucks, bicycles, helicopters, and airplanes. These African creations prove that toys don't need to be "high-tech" to be enjoyable. African games, too, can be played without any special equipment. Many African games are played with pebbles on a "board" of patterns that are drawn on the ground. Storytelling, riddlesolving, and games using animals are some other forms of play that cost no money and have no parts to break or lose. All children, whether in Africa or elsewhere in the world, are all equipped with the one essential thing needed to play: imagination.

✳ A helicopter push-toy fashioned from wire is just one of the many kinds of toys commonly found in Africa.

Play Is Social: Listening to the Griot

Performing or listening to music can be a kind of play. In many African cultures, everybody is a musician. When the Venda people of South Africa make music, there are no passive listeners; everyone joins in, singing and clapping hands. While they may often be playful, music and dancing are also serious and important to African communities. The Mangbetu people of Zaire judge a person's intelligence by his or her skill as a dancer. When a new Mangbetu chief is named, he must win a following through his dancing abilities.

✳ Musicians from the Bobo tribe of Upper Volta perform outside for the townspeople of Kuombia.

Mandinka musicians of West Africa, called *griots*, do much more than sing and play. Through their songs, griots are also storytellers, reporters, genealogists, and historians. Moving from town to town, singing and playing, a griot spreads the latest news, tells old tales, traces family trees, recounts local history, and comments on politics or current events. For children and adults, listening to griots spin tales is a relaxing leisure activity that is also educational. In medieval Europe, roving musicians called troubadors played a similar role. These wandering minstrels travelled around, singing of the latest gossip and news, telling stories, and commenting on social life. Like the medieval troubadour, the African griot spreads knowledge from place to place, teaching culture and history to the young. He also carries with him a shared language, culture, and point of view. This is sometimes called "oral tradition" because the knowledge and folklore are not written down, but pass from one generation to the next by word of mouth. Listening to the griot is a form of recreation with cultural benefits. Oral tradition helps to connect people with their past and present, and reinforces the heritage that gives a community its unique identity.

Play Helps Us to Learn: A Mathematical Game

In Africa, one of the ways children learn mathematics is through play. Kpelle children in Liberia play *tiang-kai-sii*, a counting game in which twenty-five stones are laid out in a line. While holding his breath, the player must count them out loud while touching each in succession. The counting games of older Kpelle children grow more complicated. In *kpa-keleng-je*, one stone is chosen from several rows while a player's back is turned. That player has to guess which stone is "the one" by asking questions of the others, who can move the stones around in between questions. The trick is for the player whose back is turned to keep track of the sequence in memory, and find the chosen stone by a process of elimination.

The African game of *mancala*, also called *wari*, is one of the oldest and most popular games in the world. Different versions of

＊ Members of the Mongandu tribe of Mbotolongo, Zaire, play ngola, a board-
and-counting game similar to mancala and wari.

this board game are played all over Africa, going by many names.
Mancala (an Arabic word meaning "transferral") is usually
played on a wooden board carved with two rows of six or more
holes, but it can be played without a board by scooping out
holes in the sand. The game involves moving stones or seeds
around the board and trying to capture a majority of them (see
"How to Play Wari," which follows). The basic game is thousands of years old, but today there are many different ways of
playing it. Some anthropologists have even tried to trace past
relations among different peoples according to their style of
playing this game.

Although the rules are fairly simple, the game is one of the
most mathematically complex ever created. Traditionally,
mancala was one of the ways Africans learned counting and
arithmetic. Part of the game's appeal is that it can be played
at many different levels of skill. It may be played by small children as a casual game of chance, or by grown men as a game of

How to Play Wari

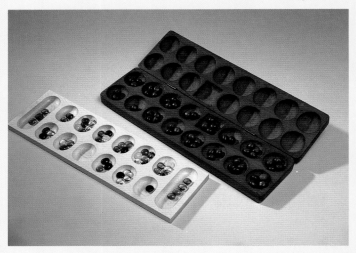

❋ A commercially made wari board and a Kenyan mancala board.

Mancala, a game that dates back to ancient Egypt, is played in many different versions throughout Africa and the world. This version, called wari, comes from the Asante people of Ghana. The wari board has fourteen indentations or cups: six on each player's side, plus one on each end for pieces that are captured during the game. At the start, each of the twelve main cups holds four "seeds" (or stones, nuts, marbles—anything that fits.) Player Number One empties any one of his cups and, moving counter-clockwise, distributes or "sows" one piece into each of the next four cups. Pieces continue to be distributed throughout the board as players alternate taking turns.

Each player tries to capture all the seeds from the opponent's side of the board. If a player drops his last seed into an empty cup on his own side, he captures all his opponent's seeds in the opposite cup. The game is over when a player cannot move because his side of the board is empty. The player with seeds remaining on his own side adds them to his reservoir of captured seeds. The player with the most seeds in his reservoir at the end wins the game.

great strategy and prestige. The Igbo tribe of Nigeria called their version *okwe*, after the name of the tree whose seeds they use as counters. In his book *My Africa*, Igbo writer Mbonu Ojike said of okwe:

> It is an adult's game, and when it is in process no one talks.... Sometimes a champion is tied up until his wife comes home, overturns the board, and says: 'Leave that nonsense thing and come home for dinner.'

Fun and Leisure: Simple Games, Sophisticated Skills

Simple games to pass the time can be a lot trickier than they seem. Many African children's games involve hiding objects. Dagon children in Mali play the ancient hide-and-seek game of *sey*. To play, two concentric circles are drawn on the ground, and each player digs three holes on his or her side. One player conceals a small pebble in one of the holes while filling them with sand. Calling "Come out, come out!" or reciting a magical phrase, the other players try to guess which hole contains the pebble. This seemingly easy game requires a sophisticated mastery of sleight-of-hand, in order to fool the other players. Sey is quite similar to the various forms of "shell games" found throughout the Americas and Europe, which also center around concealment, guessing, and sleight of hand.

Another simple game that demands great skill is *akhue*, named for the seeds used as marbles in Benin. It is played by both children and adults, often before crowds of intensely interested spectators. Three parallel lines drawn in the sand are crossed by five to seven lines drawn at right angles. One seed is placed at each intersection of the lines. Another seed, called the "captain," is placed at the end of each side (or "house") as a last line of defense. By throwing stones, seeds, or marbles, each house tries to knock out all the akhue of the opposing house. Tension builds when one house is down to its "captain," which is the most difficult of all to hit. When it is finally struck, the crowd applauds the winning side, dancing for joy and carrying the winning striker on their shoulders. Some akhue players, acclaimed in their youth for winning legendary hard-fought games, have become highly revered and have gone on to become popular rulers.

The Social Environment and the Natural Environment

Masai boys of East Africa grow up living, working, and playing in a special relationship to others born in the same generation. As small children, they play exclusively with the other members of their special social groups, known as age-grades. By playing

✳ Children on the archipelago of Seychelles—off the coast of Africa—enjoy playing on the sandy beach.

together, children try on adult roles and discover their environment. In one Masai game, children test limits, tempt fate, and strengthen skills by placing rocks on the back of a sleeping rhinoceros. Whoever wakes up the rhino with the last rock is the obvious loser (and the one who must run the fastest)! This challenging game teaches important Masai skills of stealth and courage that will be used later in hunting.

The members of each Masai age-grade continue to rely on each other as teenagers, when they pass through coming-of-age ceremonies and become young warriors and cattle herders. They will remain together for the rest of their lives as they move through adolescence, adulthood, and old age as a group. The bonds of friendship, formed in childhood play, last a lifetime and cement the basic organization of Masai society.

Many of the games people play reflect the environment in which they live. Children living in the rainforest may climb the large trees that grow there, while children in fishing villages may play games that involve miniature nets and traps. Bagara Arabs in the arid desert of the Sudan play a game called *li'b el merafib* ("hyena"), which highlights the importance of water and wildlife in the harsh desert environment. The "board" is a spiral groove drawn in the sand and marked off with some fifty or more holes. The "village" sits at the outer edge of the spiral and the "well" is in its center. Every hole symbolizes a day's journey from the village to the well and back again. Each player has a stone counter which is his "mother," and there is one extra stone called the "hyena." Players move the stones by rolling dice or throwing sticks. The first player to get his mother to the well wins the hyena. Once the mothers reach the well, they draw the water they need to wash their family's clothes. Then their "children" must get them safely back to the village. But the hyena, after drinking at the well, runs at double speed and eats any mothers it passes! Players whose mothers get "eaten" by the hyena are the butt of many good-natured jokes. Like many games, the rules and skills involved in li'b el merafib are tied to the skills and experiences that are a part of survival in that environment.

4

Europe and the Middle East

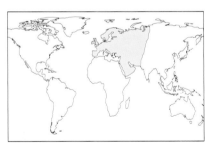

The European continent is the western part of the great Eurasian land mass. It stretches from the Atlantic Ocean in the west to the Ural Mountains and the Bosporus River in the east, and from the North Sea southward to the Mediterranean. Europe also includes the British Isles and the Scandinavian countries of Sweden, Norway, Denmark, and the Netherlands. Russia and Turkey are considered to be partly in Europe and partly in Asia. In this chapter we also include the part of southwestern Asia known as the Middle East. The Middle East includes Iran, Iraq, Saudi Arabia, Jordan, Syria, and Israel.

Geographically, this part of the world is extremely diverse. It contains many different climates—from the hot, dry sands of

✳ Opposite: Boys play an action-filled game of rugby in Great Britain.

Global Play: The Olympic Games

❋ The Olympic torch and olive branch are passed during an official ceremony.

In ancient Greece, festivals celebrating patriotism, religion, and athletics were held every four years. These games grew from a 200-yard foot race into a nationwide amateur spectacle called the Olympiad. The first Olympics featured sporting contests between the Greek city-states, as well as competitions in music and the other arts. The ancient Greeks kept their calendar according to the four-year spans between Olympic games.

About a hundred years ago, French educator Baron Pierre de Coubertin revived the ancient Greek idea of the Olympiad. The modern Olympic Games promote athletics, fitness, and international unity through friendly competition. Every two years (summer games and winter games alternate), young athletes of many nations strive for excellence and achievement in this international festival of sports and culture. All the participants play by the same rules, and all are given the same chance to win. The common language of sport and competition unites people from all over the world with a common purpose: to be the best.

Today, in the age of satellite television, the Olympic Games are truly global. The true spirit of the games is not only the competition among nations, but also the desire of individuals to achieve excellence, to push the limits of their ability, and to celebrate humanity. Olympic athletes give their all to test themselves against the best in the world, to bring honor to their countries and themselves by being the best. Using only their bodies, minds, and willpower, Olympic athletes compete in the most fundamentally human ways for all the world to see.

Arabia to the icy fjords of Scandinavia; altitudes from the alpine tundra of Switzerland to below-sea-level caves in The Netherlands; and human settlements of all kinds and sizes, from big cities to rural villages to sparsely populated deserts.

Culturally, Europe and the Middle East are equally diverse, with many languages and religions in a relatively small area. Over the long, rich history of these regions, cultures have left their marks on each other. Even today, for instance, traces of ancient Rome remain in Britain and France, and the influence of the Turkish Ottoman Empire is felt in Greece and eastern Europe. Many games of this region still show the influences of ancient and historical trade routes, conquests, and migrations throughout Europe, the Middle East, and beyond.

Kinds of Play: Indoor and Outdoor Games

Games in Europe and the Middle East are as varied as the cultures the two areas contain. Games may be played just to pass the time, during the day or night, in good weather or bad. Some games, like Europe's most popular sport of football (known as soccer in America), are played outdoors on large fields, while others are played indoors on a small tabletop. Many indoor games are miniature versions of outdoor games, in the same way that ping-pong resembles a scaled-down version of tennis. Even outdoor games may be simplified versions of sports requiring more space, players, or equipment, such as the

✳ Young Catalan boys play a game of stick hockey in Llavorsi, a town in the Pyrenees Mountains of Spain.

American street stickball games that are modeled loosely on baseball. Some popular board games, like chess, can reproduce whole battlefields in a single square foot.

Generations of English boys have played an interesting game called "kit-cat" (or the similar games "tip-cat" and "cudgel"). Three boys stand in front of small holes in the ground, holding sticks. The opposing team pitches small pieces of wood (the "cats") at them. The boys holding the sticks use them to bat the "cats," then run to dip the stick in each of the holes. A game called "kit-cat" is a smaller version of the grown-up and very popular English sport of cricket, which has much in common with American baseball.

Ball Games in Italy and France

In addition to football (soccer), which is by far the most popular sport in Italy (and the most popular sport in the world), Italians are fond of other games played with balls. The Italian game of *bocce*, descended from ancient Greek and Roman ball games, is an ancestor of bowling. Players bowl in a curved, bordered alley, trying to land their balls as close as possible to the target ball, the *pallino*. A favorite leisure time activity for Italians of all ages, bocce provides an easy-paced opportunity to relax, chat, and socialize.

In France, older men play a similar game called *boules* (or *petanque*) in cafes during the evenings or in village squares during the day. Boules can be played either individually or in teams—and a good deal of strategy and tactics are involved. A true boules player is thought to reach his prime only after the age of forty, when he has acquired sufficient strength and experience. These mostly relaxed and informal games inspire fanatical devotion among local enthusiasts. Any reasonably level ground can become a playing field, even in the middle of pedestrian traffic. Games became more organized around 1920, but a round of boules remains a social occasion where a casual, joking atmosphere still prevails.

In the game of *quilles*—another European form of bowling— players try to knock down pins with a ball attached by a rope or

chain to a tall post. In earlier versions, sheep's bones or a large egg-shaped ball called a "cheese" were thrown. It was this form of bowling, brought by Dutch colonists to America in the 1700s, that became the popular game now played in American bowling alleys all across the country.

Another bowling game is also still played in France, the simplest and rowdiest of all: barrel rolling. A hundred years ago in Paris, strong men would race huge wine barrels down the boulevards and cobblestone streets during festivals while onlookers cheered. A really good roller could manage two barrels at once. Umpires had the challenging task of deciding whether collisions were deliberate or the result of flying debris churned up by the rolling kegs.

Some games are not limited by the size of the playing field or the number of players. In Turkey, Anatolian peasants play *holani*, an ancient form of hockey that resembles a freewheeling lacrosse match. Using curved sticks, players try to knock the holani (a hard piece of wood) into the opponents' goal. The rough-and-tumble contests often go on from sunrise to sundown. Part of the fun of holani is that the game is basically a free-for-all. There are no time limits or boundaries, few or no rules, and any number of people can play at a time—up to several hundred on a side!

In smaller crowds and tighter city spaces, board games and other indoor pastimes are played. Table games are widespread indoor favorites, from pubs to rooming houses and inns. Many of these games involve pushing an object toward a goal at either end, like miniature versions of football or hockey. In Yemen, for example, after helping their parents work in the marketplace, children often get together with their friends to play *caroms*, which is a pocket billiards game for two players. This game, which probably came from northern Africa, is a favorite in southeast Asia and China as well as in the Middle East. Each

player gets nine discs of either black or white. The discs, along with a red queen, are arranged in a circle in the center of a square board or diagram scratched in the ground. The players take turns shooting a "striker" disc at the discs in the center. Each player tries to knock his own discs or the queen into pockets at the corners of the board. In North America and Great Britain, billiard halls are places where adults commonly relax and enjoy each other's company over an interesting, skillful game with a leisurely pace. Similarly, Yemeni children who work for a living also have a chance to relax, socialize and just have fun by playing the related games of caroms.

Nard is an ancient Arabic board game played in Iran and the Middle East. The basic object is for players to race pieces, or counters, around a board and cast them off the board when they safely reach the end of a circuit. Legend has it that the game was invented by an Indian wise man who based it on a calendar. The board had twenty-four points for the hours in a day (the twelve points on each side also represented the months). The thirty pieces stood for the days of the month, a pair of dice symbolized day and night, and the seven dots on the die represented the known planets and the days of the week. Nard is at least 1,200 years old, although early forms of it existed some 5,000 years ago. It is related to games played in China and Japan, as well as to the Roman game of tables, which became a favorite of the upper classes in medieval Europe. The popularity of tables spread to all walks of life. For a few centuries the church waged a campaign against the game, which was said to corrupt morals, but tables proved so addictive that even clergymen began to play! By the seventeenth century, the game of tables (then called *tric-trac* in the Middle East) was known in England by the familiar name of backgammon. When English settlers colonized North America, they, in turn, brought with them many customs and games from their homeland, including the popular backgammon.

The knucklebones of sheep or other animals have been used for thousands of years to gamble and predict the future. The game known as knucklebones was spread across Europe by Roman soldiers, but similar games have been played throughout the world for thousands of years. One modern version played throughout Europe, the Middle East, and the rest of the world is the familiar game of jacks. In this schoolyard favorite, players bounce balls and throw and catch the bones or jacks while picking them up to make "figures"—ones, twos, and so on. Among the Greenland Eskimo, the figures of the bone game are elaborate symbols of people, animals, houses, and kayaks.

Play Is Social: Skipping Games and Singing Games

Singing games, once enjoyed by adults in Europe, are now played mainly by girls between seven and nine years old. Some of the most common types are ring dances, skipping songs, clapping games, and matchmaking songs. Many are old rhymes whose origins and original meanings have been forgotten, yet children have continued to make up new verses. "London

✳ Young girls play jumprope in Anatolia, Turkey.

✳ Greek boys play a game of "blind man's bluff" in the small town of Komotini.

Bridge," one of the best-known games in the English language, has its roots in medieval society. (In Africa, children play an identical game called "Arches," except that the players are lions and leopards, and instead of a falling bridge, the collapsing arms represent an animal trap.) Another age-old rhyme, the nursery favorite "Ring Around the Rosey," probably began as a European May festival dance created to greet the spring. In some early versions, in place of the words "Ashes, ashes" is a sneeze: "Ah-choo, ah-choo"—upon which all fall down!

Fun and Leisure: Changing Patterns of Work and Play

In the nineteenth century, the industrial revolution in England dramatically changed the patterns of work and play just as it did in North America. As large factories were developed, many people left the countryside to work in cities. The long, regular hours of factory labor clearly separated work from free time. One result of this new daily structure for time was the modern idea of "leisure," meaning special activities designed to relax and entertain that were strictly separate from work. As industry spread throughout Europe, leisure activities became more organized, bringing variety and relief to the routine of people's daily working lives. As part of the boom in leisure time, spectator sports throughout Europe have grown tremendously. Today, for instance, professional soccer leagues in Britain inspire clubs of fanatical supporters who spend weekends following their favorite teams all over Europe.

In the Middle East, industrialization has been slower and more uneven. In many places, older cultural patterns still persist, and the rhythms of life are less structured and hurried. In some Middle Eastern countries, like Egypt, modern city life exists side by side with more traditional ways. Iran, Iraq, and other countries have purposely turned back to older, less western, more religious ways of life. For societies such as these—with one foot in the future and one foot in the past—the challenge is to preserve traditional practices and pastimes while taking advantage of the new technology available.

✳ A city playground provides fun for youngsters in Cairo, Egypt.

5

$\mathcal{A}$sia

The continent of Asia is a land of extremes that contains many broad cultural and geographic areas. Asia is the home of the world's coldest climate (northeastern Siberia), highest mountain range (the Himalayas), longest island chain (Indonesia), largest inland plain (the Central Asian desert and steppes), most extensive evergreen forests (the Siberian taiga), and most populous countries (China and India). The cultures of this enormous region are as diverse as the geography: large, bustling city populations of Tokyo, Delhi, and Manila; small, mountain villages of Nepal or Tibet or fishing villages of Korea or Vietnam; and roving bands of nomadic herders in Mongolia and Siberia. Many of today's cultures are deeply rooted in ancient civilizations and have remained connected to the past, unchanged, for thousands of years. Many areas have been greatly influenced by successive

59

✳ A Japanese boy practices walking through a courtyard on stilts in the Ikebukuro district of Tokyo.

waves of Hinduism, Buddhism, Islam, and Christianity. While no one element is common to all Asian cultures, many have shared roots in ancient religions.

Kinds of Play: Military Games

Throughout history, Asian peoples have had contact through trade and migration, exchanging objects, ideas, and practices, including games. Many of the world's most popular and ancient games, from fast-paced field games to slow-moving board games, have roots in Asian combat and military strategies. European chess and Chinese chess are both board games of military strategy that developed from the ancient Indian game *chaturanga*. The differences reflect the history of politics and warfare in Europe and China.

* An elderly man thinks about his next move as he plays a version of Chinese chess in the park.

Chinese chess is laid out something like the familiar European version, but the two sides are divided from each other by a line across the middle of the chessboard representing the Yellow River. Chinese chess pieces also move differently. The Chinese chess set has emperors instead of kings, mandarins instead of queens, elephants instead of bishops, and chariots instead of rooks or castles. In addition, each side has two cannons, powerful pieces that jump over the heads of other pieces in much the same way that real cannons are fired over the heads of soldiers. (Cannons are appropriate to Chinese chess, since gunpowder was invented in China.) In European chess the military goal is to entrap the opponent's king in checkmate. Chinese chess has a similar object, but the emperors are confined to "fortresses" where they are vulnerable to attack. Protecting the emperor is an important part of all offensive moves. The widely spaced pawns provide no shelter; elephants are helpful but cannot cross the river. The critical task of protecting the emperor falls mainly to the mandarins, who are also confined to the fortress. The emperor survives by hiding in the fortress and escaping at the last minute, sometimes lulling the opponent into overconfidence.

Both Chinese and European chess are games of pure mental skill and strategy in which chance plays no part. Chess games are enjoyed by young and old alike, who sharpen their skills of logic, foresight, and adaptability. From the casual matches of beginners to the most advanced tournaments of masters, chess players hone their abilities over a lifetime of experience and use the skills they hone to better survive in life.

Another military-based game, *kabaddi*, is popular in India and other parts of south Asia. It is a highly organized form of tag in which players must run and hold their breath for long periods of time. The game is a bit like such open-ended team battles played in the United States as "color war" or "capture the flag," but with several unique twists. Like most kinds of tag, kabbadi requires no equipment and can be played on many different surfaces. Two teams of twelve players each, matched according to age and weight, occupy opposite sides of the field. Seven players from each side are allowed on the field at a time; the others are reserves who enter the game as substitutes. Each side takes turns sending raiders into the opposing side's territory. The raider is like the "it" in the game of tag. As he or she runs, each raider must quickly repeat the word "kabaddi" while tagging as many opponents (or "anti-raiders") as possible and returning to the home territory—all before he or she runs out of breath! The anti-raiders use various defensive strategies, such as trying to trap the raider in a far corner of the field while evading the tag. Today kabaddi is a very disciplined sport, played by thousands of local teams who compete in nationally organized tournaments.

✳ Young shepards play a coin-tossing game in Uttar Pradesh, India.

Theater as Play and Leisure

✳ Colorful shadow puppets from Bali, Indonesia.

In Indonesia, as in many countries throughout Asia, people enjoy the theater for its leisure and entertainment value as well as for the cultural messages embodied in the productions. On the Indonesian island of Java, the highly developed art of shadow puppets has entertained for centuries. Whole villages gather for all-night performances of shadow-puppet plays. For performances, flat, intricately designed leather puppets are manipulated against a screen lit from behind, so that the audience in front sees the moving black shadows of the puppets against a white background. But the real star of the show is the *dalang*, a highly skilled master puppeteer. All night long he prays and sings, gracefully moving the puppets about, playing all the characters with his voice, narrating, and conducting a large orchestra of gongs and xylophones (collectively called a *gamelon*).

The shadow play is an event for the whole community. The audience of children and adults moves around freely, talking and laughing, sleeping or eating, drifting in and out through the night. While the shadows of the puppets can only be seen from the front of the screen, many people prefer to sit behind where they can watch the dalang and the musicians at work.

For the children and adults in the audience, a shadow play is part social occasion, part entertainment, and part lesson in history and morality. Typically, the plays trace the epic journey of a hero who must struggle with demons, battle against enemies, and outsmart political foes for a righteous cause. In the early morning hours, the sleepy audience stirs as great clashing battles are played out. As dawn breaks, the hero finally triumphs, but his victory is never final. The Javanese believe that both good and evil always exist and that each person may be partly good and partly bad. The incomplete triumph of the hero reminds the audience of the need for balance in all things and sets up the next installment of the shadow play, thus ensuring that the play continues.

As children grow up, they experience forms of theatrical drama intended mainly for adults. The world-famous Chinese Beijing opera originally developed as a favorite form of entertainment for the royal class. Actors perform on a bare stage, playing civil or military officials. They sing in high-pitched nasal voices while flutes, lutes, drums, and cymbals provide an exciting clash and clatter. The actors wear colorful costumes and makeup that represent different types of characters. The traditional patrons of the Beijing opera were nobles and warlords. Today, this court tradition has become urban entertainment, appealing especially to literate and wealthier Chinese.

In Tibet, opera is a popular rural entertainment performed outdoors under large tents. Tibetan opera, called *lhamo*, was originally performed by monks. Later, it became a kind of story-theater performed by travelling companies with music and masks. Dances, songs, and dialogue are accompanied by cymbals, drums, and other

✳ A performer in the Beijing opera.

instruments. Each character in the play is known by his or her special costume, mask, and dance rhythm. Every opera includes opening and closing dances by dancers portraying hunters or fishermen, goddesses who represent the first lhamo performers, and the Tashio Chopa, an old man who brings good fortune. For rural Tibetans living in the isolated Himilayan mountains, the appearance of a visiting lhamo troupe at the New Year's festival is one of the high points of the year.

Kathakali is a dance-drama performed in the state of Kerala in southwestern India. Like Tibetan opera, it began as a sacred tradition but is now performed more for entertainment. Dancers perform all night, accompanied by drums, cymbals, and a pair of singers who act as storytellers. As in Beijing opera, Kathakali characters are identified by their makeup. Heroes are painted bright green and wear jewelled headdresses, while demons have large red and white mustaches. The Kathakali dancer uses a special language of gesture, moving his hands and eyes in graceful patterns with precise emotional meanings. Every motion and facial expression tells the audience exactly what he is feeling. Like a skilled athlete and ballet dancer combined, a Kathakali artist undergoes disciplined training exercises and is judged by his strength, endurance, and precision of movement. As they watch a skilled performer, the audience feels the powerful emotions that the dancer portrays and learns through symbolism important morals and values of Kerala society.

✳ A teacher leads her class in an outdoor game at an elementary school in Tae Song Dong, South Korea.

In Afghanistan and Central Asia, the rough-and-tumble equestrian sport of *buzkashi* resembles a wilder form of polo, rugby, or pato (see Chapter 2). Buzkashi is said to be based on mounted defense strategies that were used against raids by Mongol horsemen. Rough, rocky ground is preferred, and riders carry whips with which they may strike their opponents. Instead of striking a ball, riders must scoop up a goat or calf (it is ritually slaughtered and stuffed beforehand) without dismounting. Goals are scored by delivering the goat to the "circle of justice" in the middle of the field while opponents try to take it away. Large crowds gather for championship buzkashi matches, which can go on for more than a week. For some Afghans, the game recalls a proud history of powerful warlords on horseback. For others, buzkashi represents all-out competition in politics and social life, and the intense battle for control of the game is considered a battle for status and power.

Play Is Social: Growing Up in Afghanistan

The games of small children in Afghanistan are much easier and safer than buzkashi. As young Afghans grow up, they develop physical, mental, and social skills gradually. From the age of four, boys challenge one another to simple head-butting contests and wrestling matches. Small boys and girls love to play "saddle-bags," in which one child (the "horse") gets down on all fours and two others balance themselves on the back of the first. When the load is balanced, the "horse" carries them on its back. Slightly older children play a local version of kabbadi in which two teams take opposite sides of the field. Players take turns shouting "kabbadi" and running between the two groups. If a player crosses the center line without being caught, one of the opponents must then join his side. The game continues until all players are on the same side.

Up to about age fifteen, Afghan children enjoy playing "boy with the stone," in which two teams face off across a line. The leader walks behind one of the lines and touches the hand of each player with a small stone while singing: "The boy I gave the pebble to has gone to pray, his prayer is lofty and long." During this song, he secretly places the stone in the hand of a player, who must run to the other side without getting caught. In "needle and thread," another version of the same game, players stand in a circle. One player is chosen as the "needle" and another as the "thread." The "needle" dodges in and out of the circle while the "thread" tries to catch him—just as in the Chinese game of "cat and mouse."

A popular game among older children and teenagers in Afghanistan is "playing thief." Each side of a matchbox is given a title such as king, policeman, farmer, commander, minister, or thief. Shouting "Who am I?", each player throws the box in the air and takes the title that lands face up. The farmer reports a stolen horse to the commander, who sends the policeman to catch the thief. The policeman brings the thief to the minister, who sends him to the king. All the players then hold court to decide on the thief's guilt or innocence, and either

Pachisi

Pachisi, the national game of India, has been played for more than 1,400 years. In the sixteenth century, the emperor Adkbar is said to have played the game while sitting in the middle of a giant marble board, ordering female slaves to stand and move as game counters! Pachisi is a favorite leisure pastime at all levels of Indian society. A version of the game became popular in England about a hundred years ago, and is widely played in Canada and the United States today.

The game is played on a cross-shaped board, usually made of embroidered cloth or velvet. Two or three can play, or four players in teams. Six cowrie shells are used as dice, and each player has four counters. (The name of the game comes from a word meaning "25", which is the highest possible throw of the cowrie shells.) The goal is to be the first player to move one's counters around the board and into the middle (*char-koni*).

Throws of the cowries are scored in the following way: If the six shells land with two to six mouths face up, the player moves from two to six spaces accordingly. If only one shell lands mouth up, the player moves ten spaces and gets another throw; and if none land mouth up, the player moves twenty-five spaces plus another throw. Each piece begins in the char-koni and moves down the middle of the player's arm of the cross. It then proceeds counter-clockwise along the sides and finally back to the char-koni (but it can only complete its journey home by an exact throw). Only one piece may be moved per throw. Players may capture enemy pieces by landing exactly on an occupied square. The captured piece starts over again from the char-koni, while the capturing player gets an extra turn. After a player's opening move, the rest of his pieces (including captured pieces) may only enter the board on a throw of six, ten, or twenty-five. At the end of each arm of the cross is a "castle" where a piece may safely remain until the player throws a twenty-five. Pieces cannot be doubled on castle squares.

When playing in teams, partners will try to help one another by blocking or capturing their opponents' pieces. If one player reaches the end, he can elect to complete a second circuit of the board in order to help his partner. Another popular version of pachisi, called *chausar*, has no castle squares and is played with dice instead of cowrie shells.

punish him or let him go. In this game, players on the verge of adulthood explore their culture's social roles and rules, as well as the commonly held notions of power, fairness, and justice.

Play Helps Us to Learn: The Japanese Game of Go

A favorite pastime in Japan is the ancient game of go, a contemplative game of strategy for two players. Go originated more than 2,000 years ago in China and is yet another military-style game, often compared with chess. But go is both more elegantly simple and more mathematically complex than chess. The go board consists of nineteen horizontal and nineteen vertical lines, which intersect at 361 points. One player uses white stones and the other black stones. The players take turns placing stones on the points. If a stone is surrounded by enemy pieces, it is "enclosed" and removed from the board. From this basic set of rules, endlessly complex possibilities are generated and an inexhaustible variety of game situations are created as stones are added. Empty points next to a stone are known as "freedoms." When a stone has only one freedom, it is in a threatened position. Students spend a lifetime learning the art of go, and masters are held in high esteem. The complex reasoning and mathematical skills required to excel at go are also academic skills that better enable young Japanese students to perform well in school. The relationship between games such as go and school are, of course, no mere coincidence.

Fun and Leisure: High-Tech and Live Action

In contrast to the formal, structured game of go, other Asian pastimes include the more informal, unstructured activities played in the villages, countrysides, and even city streets. For centuries, games involving real animals have entertained and amused people throughout Asia. In the adult world, horse racing, cockfighting, and several other wagering sports actively involve humans as spectators and animals as "players." Children everywhere also love to play with animals. In the Philippines, children catch insects for grasshopper-jumping races, cricket-chirping contests, armadillo-bug unrolling, and spider fights. Filipino kids—just like kids in rural North America—have fun catching fireflies in jars, then turning out the lights and seeing whose jar lights up first. The fun of games with live animals is partly in the hunt, partly in the fascination with the animal world, and partly in the unpredictability of the animals themselves.

Another popular Asian game with roots that reach back centuries has been raised from a popular pastime played in the village streets to a regulated, international tournament. For at least 600 years, young and old throughout the southeast Asian nation of Malaysia have competed and celebrated with an intricately woven, hollow ball called a *sepak raga* ("sepak" means "kick" and "raga" means "ball"). The sepak raga is woven of rattan in interlocking star patterns with open spaces for easy gripping. Traditional sepak raga players compete by standing, six or seven men at a time, inside a chalk circle about 50 feet (15 meters) across. Though players prefer to hit the ball with the sole of their foot, using elbows, knees, and shoulders is also allowed. Using hands, however, is strictly prohibited. With acrobatic skill, players kick or hit the ball in the air to another player, keeping it off the ground as long as possible, much like the American game of hacky sack.

For centuries, sepak raga and regional variations of the game have entertained people in Malaysia, Thailand, Burma, and other parts of southeast Asia. Often a featured highlight of village feasts, teams compete against each other, counting the number of hits made within a thirty-minute time limit. The team with the most hits is deemed champion and its members are respected as local heroes. Sepak raga heroes have been revered for centuries. In fact, legends tell of a renowned fourteenth-century Malay ruler who amazed audiences by keeping the ball in the air for over 200 kicks!

In response to the widespread popularity of the game, an official sepak raga association was founded in Malaysia in 1960. The association adapted the game slightly, adding a net (known as the *jaring*) to the center of the court and

✳ Sepak raga balls are made of tightly woven rattan and are kicked by players who try to keep them in the air.

introducing a slightly larger ball. Renamed a *bola raga*, this ball is heavier and larger because it is formed from three woven layers, as opposed to the traditional hollow, single layer sepak raga. The association also established formal regulations for play, which dictate the rules of the game, appropriate uniforms, standard methods for constructing the ball, even proper player courtesy!

✳ Pachinko players crowd the machines at a playing parlor in Tokyo, Japan.

Since the association was founded, international competitions have grown and teams from Thailand, Malaysia, Burma, and elsewhere compete in large tournaments. Meanwhile, both children and adults still enjoy the friendly competition of a local game, hoping one day to compete with their compatriots for the prized title of international champions!

While some ancient games are modernized for the purpose of international play, altogether new games arise out of new technologies. One high-tech Japanese favorite reflects the hustle and bustle of modern city life. Crowds of Japanese teenagers frequent *pachinko* parlors, where they play fast-moving games on noisy items that resemble a mixture of a pinball machine, a slot machine, and a computer. The jangle and buzz of the pachinko parlor is an integral part of the fast-paced life of Tokyo and other big Japanese cities.

Whether chasing fireflies, battling a pachinko machine, or participating in international ball tournaments, leisure time in Asia is filled with games and play that bring people together. As with most play, these activities enable people to hone special skills, test themselves, and to learn more about their place in society through special interaction.

6

Australia and the South Pacific

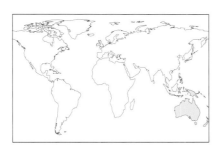

Australia is the world's largest island. It is also the only country that is, by itself, a distinct continent. For thousands of years, Australia was inhabited primarily by native peoples, called Aborigines, which included the Aranda, Wurora, Tiwi, and the Huli.

It wasn't until 1642 that the first Europeans—namely the Dutch—landed and explored the region in detail. By 1770, Captain James Cook charted the eastern coast and claimed it for Britain.

The group of islands collectively known as New Zealand were first inhabited by the Maoris, a Polynesian people believed to have first settled the region in the ninth century, A.D. Early European contacts followed the same timeline as neighboring Australia, which experienced its first European settlements in the 1640s.

✳ Opposite: A crowd enjoys the excitement of a summer horse race in Birdsville, Australia.

More than 10,000 islands—collectively known as Oceania— dot the world's largest body of water, the Pacific Ocean. Most of the larger islands are scattered in clusters throughout the western Pacific, separated from other island groups by hundreds or thousands of miles of open water. Pacific islanders, highly skilled sailors and navigators, spread out and maintained trade and social relations across vast stretches of ocean. Each of the island peoples has developed a unique culture.

Kinds of Play: Adapting Imported Games

Although they have traditionally been isolated from other cultures and have developed many indigenous games of their own, residents of Oceania have adapted imported games to their already developed native traditions. In New Zealand, for example, children that are descended from British settlers play many games that came from England. Native Maori children make up pastimes combining imported English games, like knuckle-bones, with more traditional Maori play activities that are similar but have fewer rules. Australians adapted football to the wide-open spaces of the southern continent after watching English and Irish rugby matches. Because it was first played on cricket grounds, Australian football takes place on a huge oval field. This version is primarily a kicking game with lots of fast action.

✳ The traditionally British sport of lawn bowling is a popular recreation in New Zealand.

✳ In Fiji, rugby is one of the most popular of games imported from Europe.

Play Is Social: Play as Work, Work as Play

In traditional Samoa, children and adults enjoy playing games. Yet they do not think of their daily life as divided among school, work, and play. Instead, play is often wrapped up in performing useful tasks for the family and the village. Rather than imitate the world of adults by playing house or playing with dolls, Samoan children learn by doing. From an early age, they take care of their younger brothers and sisters, and help with jobs like cooking and fishing. While the smallest children often play noisy games, singing songs and dancing in circles, their slightly older sisters and brothers will watch over them, weaving flower necklaces or mats. By the age of six or seven, Samoan children master a wide variety of adult skills, from climbing trees to catching eels. Without the familiar "industrialized" distinctions between playing and other activities, Samoan life has a rhythm all its own. The play of Samoan children not only prepares them for the adult world, but is also an inseparable part of that world.

Play Helps Us to Learn: Motu Games

Motu children in Papua New Guinea play in competitive games of physical skill. These games teach skills they will need for the tasks of adult life. Motu play often imitates important adult activities like basket making, infant care, and spearfishing. Young boys and girls alike enjoy throwing the *kuru-kuru*, a kind of tall grass, at each other. Refining hand-eye coordination through the game, they gradually develop the ability to throw accurately over long distances. The string figures of Motu "cat's cradle" provide training for netmaking, and the figures that are created represent important objects and animals, such as crabs, birds, and canoes.

The sea is all-important for the Motu, who live by fishing and trading with other island groups. Children learn to swim before they learn to walk and learn sailing skills by building and racing miniature canoes. Since Motu spend a lot of time on the sea and live in houses built on stilts, they need a good sense of balance. In the game of *manu-manu* ("little bird"), one girl sings and dances on a long wooden plank while the others carry it back and forth. Boys play *evaneva* ("looking down the pole"), in which one boy walks along the outstretched, interlocked arms of the others. As he approaches the end of the line of arms, the boys at the front rush to the end and extend it, continuing until he falls off.

Winning, Losing, and Taking Turns

People in different cultures have different ideas of what it means to win or lose. Many years ago, in the Trobriand Islands, villages traditionally competed in highly ceremonial acts of warfare. These violent raids and battles played an important part in social life, affecting everything from marriages to economics. But the winners and losers were not determined by brute force alone. A delicate balance of rules and custom made sure that no one village dominated the others. To make sure enemies remained on friendly terms, large feasts were held and gifts exchanged on a regular basis.

✳ A mother and son in Hilo, Hawaii, play a Polynesian counting game that is almost identical to the Japanese game of go.

* A group of Trobriand youngsters enjoys the freedom of playing outdoors.

Traditional warfare was outlawed during the period of British colonial government. This ended the problem of violence, but it created a new problem: How could competing village groups establish their status? Trobrianders found an answer in the English colonists' game of cricket. They changed this rather leisurely English game to fit their traditional patterns of raids and battles. Their cricket matches include huge feasts—hosted by the home team—at which rival chiefs exchange gifts. Players wear elaborate uniforms and headdresses. Whenever one team scores, play halts while they celebrate and each team performs special songs and dances. In these displays, specially composed for every possible game situation, teams dramatically boast of their own playing abilities and gleefully insult the players on the other side.

The contests go on for several days in an atmosphere of tension and excitement, until the players are exhausted from their all-out effort. In the end, however, there is one unwritten rule: The home team always wins. Winners and losers are not decided on the playing field, although the games are played hard and honestly. Winning and losing are secondary to the principle of taking turns. Winning puts the home team in the other village's debt until the next rematch, when they will switch roles. Since the losers must give the winners a feast, next time they will be the home team. Social balance is maintained, and important aspects of culture are reinforced in an atmosphere of fun.

Conclusion: What Is the Future of Recreation and Play?

Tradition and change are constantly working together to renew classic forms of play. With imagination, innovation, and more sophisticated technologies, new pastimes are continually being introduced. Some—such as computer chess—are updated forms of classic ancient games. Others—like virtual reality—give recreation a distinctly high-tech, modern twist.

As societies change, attitudes toward recreation and leisure change, too. Only a few generations ago, children in both Europe and North America were expected to behave like miniature adults; today, whole industries are devoted to toys and entertainments produced just for kids. In North America, as recently as the 1930s, recreation and leisure were considered luxuries. By the 1950s, however, organized recreation was seen as a kind of "medicine" for the body and soul. Today, most people pursue recreation largely for its own sake—to entertain and relax.

In many ways, instant communications and jet travel have made the world smaller than ever. Yet, through this increased access to the world, we discover more and more about each other and are able to more easily share traditions, cultures, and pastimes with one another. In this sense, our world is growing larger. As we learn more about the wonderful diversity of our human species, we also discover the many things that unite us. We all play, but there are as many ways to play as there are players.

The future of play and recreation is up to the children of the world, the adults of tomorrow. No matter how basic or advanced the technology, the most important element in any game is the spark of human creativity and imagination. The next time you find yourself at play, take a moment to reflect on the universal and unique qualities of whatever game you choose. By thinking of the many different ways people play, you bring yourself closer to the basic human spirit of playfulness that we all share.

Glossary

age-grades In the Masai tribe of East Africa, a social group made up of boys who are born in the same generation, and who play exclusively with each other.

approach-avoidance A type of play among animals in which playmates chase each other yet have minimal physical contact.

blood sport A dangerous game in which blood is shed.

games of concealment Guessing games where players must guess where an object is being hidden.

games of chance Games in which the player or players try to guess the outcome of the game being played.

interactive electronic leisure An activity in which players sit or stand while playing video or computer games. Players must react to the images and commands on the screen before them.

military games Games in which players must use mental skills and strategy in order to win.

play-acting A non-competitive type of play that entertains an audience, or is done for recreation; also known as role-playing.

rough-and-tumble A type of rough play among animals, which involves harmless but fierce biting and scratching.

spectator sports Sports that are played for entertainment value before large crowds.

Further Reading

Aaseng, Nathan. *The Locker Room Mirror: How Sports Reflect Society.* New York: Walker & Company, 1993.

Arnold, Caroline. *Soccer: From Neighborhood Play to the World Cup.* New York: Franklin Watts, 1991.

Barrett, Norman. *Sport: Players, Games and Spectacle.* New York: Franklin Watts, 1991.

Berger, Gilda. *Violence and Sports.* New York: Franklin Watts, 1990.

Clark, Raymond C. and Jerald, Michael. *Summer Olympic Games: Exploring International Athletic Competition.* Brattleboro, VT: Pro Lingua Associates, 1987.

Glubok, Shirley, and Tamarin, Alfred. *Olympic Games in Ancient Greece.* New York: HarperCollins Children's Books, 1976.

Masciantonio, Rudolph. *Greco Roman Sports and Games.* Oxford, OH: The American Classical League, 1991.

Whitney, Alex. *Sports and Games the Indians Gave Us.* New York: David McKay, Co., Inc., 1977.

Index

Photo Credits

Page 8: O. Louis Mazzatenta/© National Geographic Society; p. 10: © Robert A. Isaacs/Photo Researchers, Inc.; p. 11: Courtesy United Nations Photo Archives; p. 12: Dean Conger/© National Geographic Society; p. 14: © Robert A. Isaacs/Photo Researchers, Inc.; p. 16: © Gerard Lacz/Peter Arnold, Inc.; p. 17: © Mitch Reardon/Photo Researchers, Inc.; p. 18: Jodi Cobb/© National Geographic Society; p. 20: Myrleen Ferguson/ Tony Stone Worldwide; p. 21 (inset): © Horace Day; p. 21: © National Geographic Society; p. 24: © Arthur Tilley/Tony Stone Worldwide; p. 27: © Bill Welch; p. 29: © Mathias Oppersdorff/Photo Researchers, Inc.; pp. 30–31: © Jim Cochrane/courtesy Canadian Office of Tourism; p. 32: © Kay Muldoon Ibrahim/courtesy United Nations Photo Archives; p. 33: © Brian Seed/Tony Stone Worldwide; p. 34: courtesy United Nations Photo Archives; p. 36: © University of Washington Photography; p. 37: Raymond Gehman/courtesy National Geographic Society; p. 38: © Victor Englebert; p. 40: photo by Richard Stum/© DMNH Photo Archives; p. 41: © Jacques Jangoux/Tony Stone Worldwide; p. 43: James P. Blair/© National Geographic Society; p. 44: photo by Richard Stum/© DMNH Photo Archives; p. 46: © John Garrett/Tony Stone Worldwide; p. 48: Tony Stone Worldwide; p. 50: © Benali-Sampers/Gamma Liaison; p. 51: © Edwin Grosvenor/National Geographic Image Collection; p. 53: © Richard Passmore/Tony Stone Worldwide; p. 54: © James L. Stanfield/National Geographic Image Collection; p. 55: © Robert Frerck/Tony Stone Worldwide; p. 56: James P. Blair/© National Geographic Society; p. 57: © Jack Fields/Tony Stone Worldwide; p. 58: David Alan Harvey/© National Geographic Society; p. 60: © Dale Boyer/Tony Stone Worldwide; p. 61: courtesy United Nations Photo Archives; p. 62: © Bachmann/Photo Researchers, Inc.; p. 63: © Brian Yarvin/Photo Researchers, Inc.; p. 64: © Emory Kristof/National Geographic Image Collection; p. 68: photo by Richard Stum/© DMNH Photo Archives; p. 69: © Steve Vidler/Leo de Wys, Inc.; p. 70: © David Austin/Tony Stone Worldwide; p. 72: © Paul Chesley/ Tony Stone Worldwide; p. 73: © Jack Fields/Photo Researchers, Inc.; p. 74: © Steven L. Raymer/National Geographic Image Collection; p. 75: © Malcolm S. Kirk/Peter Arnold, Inc.